"As you read [...] will be extre[mely...] and stirred by the content of their wisdom. Esther's life experience has taught her to view circumstances without prejudice or criticism, whether it concerns people, places, or things. She has learned to see the providence of God in every situation."

Clyde M. Shaw, Senior Pastor
Gospel Assembly Church
Jerseyville, Illinois

"I find it amazing that such a gentle woman can write such powerful prose. I witness the affect her writing has on the people around her and people in all walks of life. Her common sense and gentle nature have been guiding lights in my life personally. I'm so very lucky to be able to call 'Grammy' my mother."

Bob Reagan

"All the people who know Esther and are around her truly know that God gave us all a special gift when he made her."

Greg Miller

"Esther is always there to give love and encouragement and share her talent in personal little love stories. To be able to share her life and her stories is just a blessing to others. When you read these pages, know that the writer is one of the most genuine, loving, spiritual people you would ever meet. These words are truly from her heart and soul."

Robyn Broadway

"Esther helps me see things that I can't put into my own words. Her writings bring my feelings and emotions to the surface so healing can begin within. She looks beyond and deep into the soul."

Debbie Guess

"Having had access to some of Grammy Esther's poems, I find a collection of expressions of love admiration, comfort, wisdom, mystery, and experience by good days and bad days. I feel she has a gift from God to bless others. She truly has the hand of a ready writer."

Bessie Livsey

"Esther Miller has been graced with a God-given talent to express what many of us feel, but are not able to put into words. She has been given the gift through her words to encourage those of us who sometimes feel weak, lost, lonely, and in despair. She also possesses the ability to make us laugh with her witty and sometimes humorous look at life. She has such an appreciation for the World of Nature that God has provided us and, through her words, reminds us to look for God through His gift of Nature. If through the words of her gentle, loving, and humble spirit just one person is encouraged, the goal that God bestowed upon her with her talent will have been accomplished. Thank you, Esther Miller, for following your heart and allowing God to use you to encourage us, and may He continue to Bless You!"

Gayle Sams

"She is truly the GEM that her initials spell. She has so many facets…like the Jewel she is. Esther's poems inspire, uplift, and encourage."

Beverly Jean Lane

INSPIRATIONS, REFLECTIONS & LOVE

A poetic celebration of life by one whose heart God has touched

INSPIRATIONS, REFLECTIONS
— & —
LOVE

written by
GRAMMY ESTHER

TATE PUBLISHING *& Enterprises*

Inspiration, Reflections, and Love
Copyright © 2007 by GRAMMY ESTHER. All rights reserved.

This title is also available as a Tate Out Loud product. Visit www.tatepublishing.com for more information.

No part of this publication may be reproduced, stored in a retrieval system or transmitted in any way by any means, electronic, mechanical, photocopy, recording or otherwise without the prior permission of the author except as provided by USA copyright law.

The opinions expressed by the author are not necessarily those of Tate Publishing, LLC.

Published by Tate Publishing & Enterprises, LLC
127 E. Trade Center Terrace | Mustang, Oklahoma 73064 USA
1.888.361.9473 | www.tatepublishing.com

Tate Publishing is committed to excellence in the publishing industry. The company reflects the philosophy established by the founders, based on Psalms 68:11,

"The Lord gave the word and great was the company of those who published it."

Book design copyright © 2007 by Tate Publishing, LLC. All rights reserved.
Cover design by Elizabeth Mason
Interior design by Janae J. Glass

Published in the United States of America
ISBN: 978-1-60247-797-1
1. Christian Poetry   2. Inspirational

07.08.07

ACKNOWLEDGMENTS

First of all, I thank my Lord for allowing me to find my voice. He is my Friend and the Keeper of my soul, and because He did know me...He allowed me to realize what writing could mean to me. I could see what a wonderful tool I had in my hands. It was a tool I could use to express all those silent conversations that I had with myself and my Friend, the Lord. All I needed then was inspiration, and, of course, I needed to learn how to express the thought that had been inspired. My inspiration came when I fell in love with the Lord. Only then did I learn how to truly express the love I feel for my husband and my wonderful children and grandchildren; to savor the excitement and beauty of our natural environment; and most of all, to have the awareness and experience the depth of each and every circumstance that life presents to me daily. Anything that triggered an emotion was an inspiration for me.

A special thanks to my friend Rebecca Myers, who secretly put together the first of my yearly family poem books and has assisted me in many other writing ventures.

I am also thankful to Tate Publishing for turning up the volume on my voice. In much love, I dedicate this book of poetry and thoughts to my wonderful family and friends who love me and inspire my writings. May God smile on all of you, and may you always feel my love and prayers around you.

Grammy Esther

TABLE OF CONTENTS

Foreword 15
Midst the Morning. 19
God's Priceless Gift. 20
Why has God Chosen Me? 22
God of Miracles 24
Look Higher 26
Walk in the Rain 28
High Above My Cares 29
Existing is Change 31
Count Your Blessings 33
Rest–Rise–Dream 35
Harsh Actions. 37
The Pull of Passion. 39
This Is a Test. 41
Haunting 42
The Invisible Things 43
Excess 46
Credit Card Debt 47
Just One More Day. 48

Integrity	49
Learning Wisdom	51
Measure of Faith	545
Temperance	56
Lord, Help Me Love and Forgive	58
Humility	60
Beware of the Pot Stirrer	62
Between You and Me	64
Dead Above Ground	66
I've Danced Off With Angels	68
We Feel What We Think	70
The Hardest Prayer	72
Lord, Teach My Children	74
Is It Charity or Condescension?	76
Look for the Key	78
Have I Seen Too Much?	80
Beautiful Testing Ground	82
My Window View	83
Seeing Is Worse Than Being	84
Beautiful View	86
No Guarantees in Life	87
A Heavenly Morning	88

My Hill	89
Obedience	91
His Unseen Presence	93
What Is a Man?	95
Lord, Help Us All	97
Love Again and Again	99
The Serpent's Voice	101
My Peaceful Hilltop Home	103
The Lead Horse	104
Pastor Shaw	106
Our Pastor's Lady	108
God Is Love	110
Lord, It's Just Me	112
Life Triggers Change	114
Truth and Reality	116
Give Me Faith to Have Faith	117
Take Time	118
God's Gift of Love	119
Stay Pliable in His Hand	124
Think it Through Again	126
Heart of a Healer	128
Help Me, Doc	130

The Goat and the Electric Fence	131
Throw Caution to the Wind	134
The Person I Be	136
Lady and the Storm	137
Thanks for Making Me a Momma	138
Father's Day Blueprint	141
How Can I Say Goodbye?	143
Words	144
The Wind Is a Bully	145
Looking for Santa	147
Just Be Happy	150
Hidden Places	151
If You Live Long Enough	153
This Woman I Used to Know	155
Siblings	157
Why?	159
My Family of Separates	161
My Misty Memories	163
Mr. Hunter	165
Life's Marketplace	166
A Momma Child	168

FOREWORD

Grammy Esther is a retiree of McDonnell Douglas, where she worked as a research technician while raising a son and daughter as a single parent. Her experiences raising her children and growing up on her family farm in Missouri gave her much of the material she uses in her writing. She didn't start writing until she was in her fifties, and her memories were packed full of material. Esther lives with her husband, Charles, in Fieldon, Illinois. They live on what she refers to as "my hill-top home." Her husband encouraged her to publish her written works because he believes her writings encourage and uplift others.

Most of her poetry was written as love notes to God and her family plus some funny stories thrown in about her life as a young girl on the family farm in southeast Missouri. It goes without saying that her writings reflect her feelings about experiences at one time or another or some condition she has observed. She used writing to work through sadness, excitement, or whatever life might be pitching to her on any given day. She used her writing to encourage others when they wanted to throw in the towel; she is a natural cheerleader for the downhearted.

She was given the name Grammy by her grandchildren when they were learning to talk, and as the name Grammy Esther indicates, she loves being a mother and grandmother. She has also acquired other names such as, just Grammy, Mom-O, Grambo, Momma-Child, Gram, Mommy, Marie, and so many others.

Esther was born on May 4, 1939, during a rainstorm in her tiny family home on the outskirts of a postage-stamp-sized town called Gipsy Missouri. Because it was flooding at the same time she decided to come into the world, Esther was delivered by her father and a neighbor lady.

Ask her about her future writing, and she would tell you she plans to write until she exhausts every word in her vocabulary. She says that is because after finding her voice, writing has become a compulsion, or at least her treasured means of expressing the thought and feelings of the little girl that lives inside her.

Ask her friends and they will tell you there is no end to her. She lives in her head, and she is full of opinions, very humorous, a truth seeker, a realist, but still a dreamer, and last but certainly not least, a philosopher. As an aside to that title, her family has decided that to describe her after death, they will engrave on her tombstone, "I've been thinking about that…and…" This is something she almost always says when she hasn't thought a matter completely through or come up with an opinion that she is willing to accept as her own. Lastly, I believe she is one of those people who has been inspired by life and, in turn, inspires all those who take the time to get to know her.

I can say all this because I know them to be true; she is my mom.

Cindy Miller

MIDST THE MORNING

Midst the stillness of the morning
a soft, painted sky I see.
I am blessed to feel the splendor
the Lord has given me.

In this muted light, I feel His Glory
and His presence is all around.
I'm thankful that He lingers near
and in prayer is always found.

I close my eyes…it seems so Holy
this awesome, calming peace.
Wrapped in His love I stand in silence
while my troubles and worries cease.

GOD'S PRICELESS GIFT

The Christ child's birth is what we honor on each Christmas Day, let everyone in thanksgiving bow your hearts and pray. Our Father sent a priceless gift, the half not yet been told, but if we keep our hearts in tune the picture will unfold. God and His Son were looking down upon a fallen race, He could have simply wiped us out and never left a trace. For man, in whom He placed such hope, could never learn to stand. He always followed lust and greed and chose the will of man. Though God was sad, he still felt love, though He knew man's life was out of hand. For the people that he loved so much had failed to understand. How can I send My only Son into that world below? Is this the way—the only way—that I can truly know? The human always seems to fail and is slow to comprehend. Could there be another way to feel the ways of men? Jesus came and lived the stages that each human person grew, From babe to child, to manhood, the human ways He lived and knew. His life was always threatened, from the manger to the cross. Still He lived those pictured patterns, an example for the lost. Jesus taught them of His Father, and He stuck right to the plan. God had sent his only Son, a gift to dying man. His thanks came as brutalities that He endured without a sound.

Some beat and crucified Him, others cheering all around. When His mission was completed and everything was done, He resurrected and ascended into Heaven God's own Son. God, thank you for this priceless gift of love that set us free. It is too much to comprehend…this gift that You have given me.

WHY HAS GOD CHOSEN ME?

If I remember God watches me
like I am watching you,
then a better person I'll become
and kinder things I'll do.

If I could hide and watch myself
the way that others do,
what pictures would my life reveal
if every thought came through?

God's righteousness should be my coat
as His spirit grows within,
Christ's love my motivating force
for victory over sin.

When Jesus lived and died for me,
then ascended up above,
God declared, "Not Guilty.
Your sins are covered by His love."

He sees me differently than I do
and it makes my heart rejoice,
to hear Him speaking deep within
in that soul's soft, whispering voice.

I must remember that He called me
and seek His will, accept His grace,
then trust that He knows me better—
that I'm His child and have a place.

Each day I must try to see myself
in the way that He must see,
though I will never comprehend
why He has chosen me.

GOD OF MIRACLES

So you think you've reached the end of your rope
and dread has wrinkled your brow.
You're worried about problems that lie ahead
plus the load you are carrying now.
Your problems are cruel and they oppose you
as you wrestle them all alone.
Just remember there at the end of your rope
is where God is right at home.

When you feel you've reached the end of your rope
and your life before you is spread,
most of your dreams are already shattered,
breaking your heart and clouding your head.
You're searching for strength just to hang on
while clinching your trembling hands.
Just remember at the end of your rope
your Problem-Solver stands.

When you think you're at the end of your rope
and you don't know "which" from "what,"
just cry out to your Father in Heaven—
He cares and He faileth not.
It's not the problem He changes,
it's the outcome He switches around,
and right there at the end of your rope
is this God of miracles found.

When you think you're at the end of your rope,
you've prayed hard and no answer is heard,
you're feeling sick and racked with fear
and your image of God is somewhat blurred,
just believe that God has heard you
and trust He will make a way.
God will not fail! Your help will come!
Somewhere! Somehow! Someway!

LOOK HIGHER

Lift your thinking a little higher.
Your sight may be too low to see.
If you look, you'll be amazed what
God has given you for free.
We only see in fleeting glances,
but we should view the whole.
With closed eyes, look a little closer
and the picture will unfold.

Lift your spirits a little higher
and your blessings appreciate,
then cherish treasures that you have,
before it is too late.
Anyone can miss a blessing
sitting right before their eyes
preoccupied by life and living,
trying to be worldly wise.

Lift your spirits a little higher and look
past shadows of the day.
God will shine a light, I'm sure,
for each of us to find the way.
There is none among the living with
wealth enough to pay
for the sad, unhappy memories
that refuse to go away.

Lift your spirits a little higher and
look beyond that sorrow now.
Your pain and heartaches are too heavy;
tell despair to take a bow.
Time and life are passing by and
both will leave their mark.
Don't waste your life on broken dreams
and crying in the dark.

Lift your spirits a little higher;
love will stay when life goes wrong.
Love is such a crucial bond,
so delicate and yet so strong.
So cherish love with all your might,
it can't be bought or sold.
Love is a very special gift—
more valuable than gold.

Lift your spirits a little higher.
The Lord is always near at hand.
He's there when your life's unsettled
and hard to understand.
So let your conscience be your guide
and hold to God's unchanging hand.
Only then you'll know the path to travel
and you'll see the Master Plan.

WALK IN THE RAIN

The morning seems restless
as I walk on my hill,
no leaves to rustle
but it's noisy still.
The trees are black
and the skies are gray
as the weeds and the grass
bow their heads to pray.
No birds are flying,
all the deer hidden away,
too dreary a day
for my friends to play.
The wind is cold
and it's blowing rain,
but the beauty of my hilltop
still remains.

HIGH ABOVE MY CARES

The morning sun rose on my hill
the sky was clear and oh so blue.
The air filled up with nature's song
as my thankful heart sang out to You.

Thanks for the morning and the evening,
the vibrant dawning
and shadows of night.
Displaying the Creator's power and glory,
God's Christ…my Everlasting Light.

My hilltop is high above my cares,
at least it seems to be,
and every view seems lovelier
than those I used to see.

At dawn a small cloud filled with rain
came to wash my dusty hill.
In breathless wonder I stood there,
and its beauty paralyzed my will.

Dear God, I thank You for Your Son,
for He's given beauty to my life.
In Him my troubles bring about victory
by lessons I learned in the strife.

Inspiration, Reflections, & Love

All those battlefields bring about courage,
understanding, then power and peace.
Because after I share a sunrise with You,
my desire to quit...I release.

When the sunrise breaks upon my hill
and my will absorbed in the sky so blue,
or I'm carried away with nature's song
I find that my heart is in tune with You.

EXISTING IS CHANGE

I'm so thankful, Lord, for this gift of Life
a time to breathe, to hear, and see.
A chance to live and grow in peace,
learning to nurture Your Life in me.

The beginning of change started at birth,
then maturing changed me more.
Your Word and Spirit kept me going,
and my soul, Your love restored.

You taught me that problems are
Heaven sent,
and trials hold the seeds of success.
Difficulties are just opportunities
for self-reflection as I progress.

You teach all things increase by giving
and little is more when I share.
Learning while growing
and staying humble
promote endeavors beyond compare.

When problems arise,
consider the matter—
don't throw fits and condemn.
Opportunities and problems come to all,

but it's up to you how you handle them.
Consider the people who
make a difference,
most are just common folks who care.

Impressive credentials are
not too important,
for God blesses the efforts of
those who share.

Don't let me give up on myself or others
when life seems hopeless and all uphill.
I need You to give me courage and grace
while changing my nature
and stubborn will.

I thank You, Lord, for this
chance to change.
Thanks You for the life
You have breathed into me.
Thanks for Your Word
that gives me peace,
producing a change that others can see.

COUNT YOUR BLESSINGS

When your pockets are empty and
your cupboards are bare,
and nobody is near your troubles to share,
Count Your Blessings.
When it's hard to smile and
you're down in the dumps,
you've got muddy roads full of holes and bumps,
Count Your Blessings.
When it's a long road home
and the way is cold and far,
and you're walking 'cause there is no gas in the car,
Count Your Blessings
When your every thought is wrapped up in fear,
when you're feeling confused and nothing is clear,
Count Your Blessings.
Like a fly that is caught in a spider's web,
swinging to and fro, and all hope has fled,
Count Your Blessings.
You're sure no one cares and their dislike shows,
and you're dislocated with no place to go,
Count Your Blessings.
When you cry and not a tear will fall,
when you scream and there's no sound at all,
Count Your Blessings.
When you've searched your entire world for peace,
and you're praying your trouble

Inspiration, Reflections, & Love

and turmoil will cease,
Count Your Blessings.
When war is raging in your breast,
that stirs the beast within,
when chaos puts you to the test,
and you cry out for a friend,
Count Your Blessings.
When you're searching for objects you cannot find,
and consider leaving them all behind,
Count Your Blessings
When your pockets are empty
and your cupboards are bare,
and you need someone, your troubles to share.
Just count your blessings,
and find your peace there.

REST–RISE–DREAM

The sun is setting on my hill
it's the close of one more day.
My body is weary and needing to rest
but my furry little friends are ready to play.
They play in the dark far better than me
while hiding from prying eyes.
The deer and possums are nosing around
and a sneaky old fox is trying to spy.
The darkening shadows cover the fields
as the water mirrors the soft night light.
The shining stars light up the hillsides
as my dog and a raccoon make ready to fight.
The dog's hair is bristled, showing his teeth
growling and nudging the coon now and then.
The raccoon taunts the dog from the shadows
but then runs before the fight can begin.
I stay up all night in this world of darkness
and am awestruck by the rising sun.
Surveying the beauty of God's creations
reflections of love—yes, every one.
There in silence I hear a voice
speaking quietly in my ear.
It is soft among the morning sounds
yet loud enough for me to hear.
My Father is speaking to me,
saying, "Child, never be forlorn.

Just let your heart be set on Me
for that is where your dreams are born.
Righteousness will keep you free
and your strength will come from Me.
You truly are a dreamer, child,
and dreams become reality."

HARSH, HASTY ACTIONS

In this hustle-bustle rush-about
amid mayhem and strife,
I fear I've often failed to honor
the greater things of life.

At times evading or dodging duty
those things I should have done,
or the many times ignoring the problems
of a weary or helpless one.

There is a room I keep for memories
only accessed through my mind,
housing a diary of my whole life
with each occurrence well-defined.

Sometimes I enter and it lifts me up
and fills my heart with peace.
Sometimes it makes my heart cry out
when a haunting sadness is released.

At the time I did not understand
the price my deeds would cost.
Through eyes of youth I did not see
how anger brings such loss.

If I could be a perfect person
with only God's life shaping my soul.
I would never allow harsh, hasty actions
to cause my spirit to lose control.

My secret room holds bitter memories
of words I should have kept inside.
Echoing things my mouth spewed out
that I can't call back…though I've tried.

So when life is filled with hustle-bustle
running over with mayhem and strife,
I pray that I stop and remember this lesson
and embrace the greater things of life.

THE PULL OF PASSION

Our world is controlled by passions
by definition meaning a lot of things.
Strong emotions like love and hate
cause logic to take to the wing.

It's true we're all driven by passions
letting some pass by and others remain.
Passion implies very strong feelings
and we can choose which we entertain.

Greed is a selfish passion
taking more than you need or deserve
completely obsessed by acquiring
and obtaining things that self-serve.

If you target ill will to your fellow man
at the end it will alter your course.
Then the passion might be hatred or anger
and both are a negative force.

Don't waste your life on aggression
for hostility and fury confine.
Don't let anger enrage or provoke you
or your welfare will be undermined.

Let your passion be love and devotion
of God and your fellow man.
Take delight in helping someone in need
and make sharing your overall plan.

What is the purpose of passion?
Why does it drive us so?
Why is always a bit extreme?
Why is it always a high or a low?

THIS IS A TEST

I love You, Lord. I want to trust You
and never worry after I've prayed,
even though my roof is leaking
and all my skies have turned to gray.

You only send trials to test me
and this one hasn't come to stay.
The Word says that You love me
and Your plan is underway.

The Bible says You always try
the ones You love the best.
So when I'm scared and all alone,
I'll shout out loud, "This is a test!"

I know You won't forget me here
You love me and I'm Your child.
So through my life I'll trust You, Lord,
and hold Your hand and smile.

HAUNTING

Lord, I feel You drawing me
yet many things I fear.
You may never really speak to me
but Your voice I seem to hear.

With failures more than my successes
still I feel Your spirit near.
Like a ghost You haunt my nights,
a presence tangible and dear.

I fear I'll never prove myself
though Your perfect way is here.
I pray you help my unbelief
and keep my pathway clear.

Lord, I'm alive and so are You
and nothing I should fear.
So by Your Love, please hold me close
and dry my falling tears.

THE INVISIBLE THINGS

The driving forces in this life are things
you cannot see.
Though they appear intangible,
they're life and breath to me.
I was afraid to live my life, I felt out of control;
so fearful of the feelings that
kept torturing my soul.
There was joy and happiness,
but happy can't be seen.
Then bitterness, anger, and
hate crept in to make me mean.
If I became stressed or anxious,
it was then my temper flew.
I had no patience for myself and
absolutely none for you.
I heard people talk about Jesus,
and they said I had a soul.
All these things seemed intangible,
invisible, and cold.
It was then I found a Bible
and I sat right down to read.
I read the parable of the sower.
Jesus said His words were seed.
I thought about the things He said
and how a seed would grow.
Then I could feel a stirring

and a peace began to flow.
I told God I was afraid of Him,
but I didn't want to be.
I asked if I could be His child
and understand what I couldn't see.
Then I started talking to Him
and kept reading from His Word.
The excitement grew inside me
with everything I heard.
The Commandments God gave
Moses are a predestined strategy,
all examples of man's nature, a plan of destiny.
God wanted man to understand
the objective in His plan,
but they only saw the natural law
and used it to rule the land.
Man was created in God's own image,
but he fell and lost his sight;
yet his soul kept an awareness,
he was troubled in the night.
I thank God for troubled water,
for that was how He got to me.
I was sinking fast in a leaky boat
in the waters of humanity.
The Bible said the law was dead
and life it couldn't bring
until God's Son came as mortal man
and it made the angels sing.
Our Savior came to live and die,
explaining God's good Plan

for man's soul is quite elusive,
you can't hold it in your hand.
All these things I had envisioned
as intangible and cold.
They were in fact just invisible,
but could live there in my soul.
Now I read my Bible, smiling
and the Spirit stirs within.
I am no longer frightened,
for I've found a long lost Friend.

EXCESS

If what I have I can't take care of,
then I'm living in excess.
When I buy what I can't pay for,
it's a fact...I'm dishonest.

If I'm excessive in my spending,
I am acting superfluous.
When things I own I have no need of,
then I'm wasting God's surplus.

When other people live in shortage
while provisions ruin behind my door,
and someone needs what I am hoarding
then I'm robbing Heaven's store.

I inventory the things I've stored up,
it is another's necessity;
what I've amassed, heaped up, collected
in a stock-pile just for me.

Then if I am in my ways excessive
and cannot see a brother's need,
please reveal these things, my Father,
and gently heal my unknown greed.

CREDIT CARD DEBT

By the end of the month, everyone's broke
it's getting to be a regular joke.
This mark of America's common folk
marketing hype and, "Go for broke!"

Working two jobs, you'll learn right away.
It's easy to spend and hard to pay.
It wrinkles your brow and your hair turns gray
This "easy credit" is all one way.

You'll never be free with a crave to spend
or shop just because you get a yen,
when your need to buy puts you in a spin
then debt becomes the ultimate sin.

JUST ONE MORE DAY

I told the Lord I must say goodbye
to keep from bringing Him shame,
because He is so mighty and perfect
and I am unworthy to carry His name.
My heart nearly melted in pain
as my life started falling apart.
Then He picked me up in His Love and said,
"I love you, and I see your heart.
Others may judge by the words that you speak,
by things that you possess, or the clothes you wear,
but they never walked on the
roads that you traveled,
so your language is strange and
your thoughts they can't share.
They only see the way you appear
for you've closed the door to that internal part.
They only see the things that you do,
but I love you, and I see your heart.
So don't fear the skies as they darken above,
don't stop or bolt and run away.
Just keep on doing the things that I say.
Have faith and trust Me—Just One More Day."

INTEGRITY

Integrity is a word often heard
but quite worthless until it's applied
by people with honorable ways and motives
using righteousness as their guide.
Integrity is the highest of "Callings,"
a reflection of God in man.
It means you're always what you say
and never perform a slight of hand.
When you make a decision to do the right thing
most likely you'll find opposition.
When it's a test of integrity for you to stand
and then to defend your position.
It's one thing to say you believe in your action
but another to do the right thing.
For when others oppose, it's easy to doubt
and fail to catch the brass ring.
Even as children, we all need convictions
and not just learn words, one by one.
Integrity becomes part of our souls
by the challenging battles we've won.
Integrity needs to be put to the test
by pressures experienced in strife.
Convictions are barren if they can't survive
the refining fires of our life.
I want to be a person of principle
true to my God and my self.

Let integrity be an extension of me
something I am...not stored on a shelf.
When my life doesn't go as I plan it
and calamity repeatedly strikes,
when my true character surfaces
and bad and good are "Look-a-Likes,"
Dear God, help me examine myself,
embrace Your truth and Your ways.
Then prize integrity...the intangible force
and be virtuous all of my days.

LEARNING WISDOM

Each living person is different,
and each of us have our own ways.
By the same five senses we differ
and choose the temperament we display.

In our world filled with hatred and anger
while deflecting rejection, we hide in denial.
We're all humans with beastly natures
finding it hard to reconcile.

When I find other's values are faulty
and I judge only a few of them true
when I find that you're different than I am
then I can't or I won't accept you.

Our God wants for us something different.
He gave us His Spirit and the Life of His Son,
then covered us with His banner of love
hopeful His Spirit would ours overcome.

His Will is that we not be anxious,
for worry is pointless at best.
We can't cross a bridge before we arrive
and trying just causes distress.

Inspiration, Reflections, & Love

Problems must be handled in order
facing them one by one
but resolve or leave them before bedtime
for when worrying, sleep does not come.

We can never unscramble those eggs.
The past is forever gone.
And all those troubles in other folks' lives
will just keep us tossing till dawn.

I've met that monster, "Demon Fear,"
who controls by fear of things to come.
He keeps us bogged down in frustrations
and self is the root of them, every one.

We should cover our troubles with faith
and count our blessings big and small
For sometimes the reason for problems
is simply a wake-up call.

If we are here and speaking,
we have a new day to live as we will.
If we love and forgive, we gain peace.
If we hate, peace just slides down the hill.

Sometimes those things we wanted to say
were better just left unsaid.
For without fuel, the fire burns out,
and it's a damaging fire that is overfed.

If I can honestly examine myself,
I will more easily understand you.
If I cease from self-pity and blaming,
I will see what is really true.

If I express feelings in a loving way
and use self-control day-by-day,
if I can forgive myself and others,
then my Lord will hear when I pray.

To control myself would be wisdom,
and wisdom is thinking before I act.
This makes my actions less impulsive
and my blunders will have less impact.

I pray God will bless me with knowledge
and allow me to understand all.
But while learning I pray He gives me wisdom
and mercy if I start to fall.

MEASURE OF FAITH

Thank You, my Lord, for this measure of faith…
this wonderful gift from You.
Help me commit to and trust this faith…
not trusting in me, but in You.

Sometimes life will rock my faith,
then it is hard for me to pray
For when I'm blinded by my fear,
I start to lose my way.

Let my measure of faith be a refuge.
Let me run to You and find peace.
Make my vision a likeness of You
and let it forever increase.

Don't let me make my faith a prison
where I live in fear night and day.
Don't let me use my faith as a weapon
with its purpose to conquer or slay.

You touched my heart and my eyes, Lord,
and said by my faith it would be
That by grace through faith I could see You
and believe that You really loved me.

You have taught me to walk by faith
and believe in things that I cannot see.
You taught me the law could not give me life
but Your Word would paint pictures for me.

Now by faith I will follow Your patterns
and trust that Your favor I win.
And I won't fear the dark or life's tremors
for in faith You'll be with me until the end.

TEMPERANCE

Temperance—calm and collected.
Is it only just a word?
Records of this action are rarely seen or heard.
A condition full of quality...
dispassionate, so I'm told
With a quicker apprehension
that is neither meek nor bold.
Self-restraint—weaving no web—
a clearness of the head;
being sure your mind is working
before a word is said.
Wisdom shows us what to speak...
some words sound best unsaid.
Voicing only things we should,
leaving sleeping dogs in bed.
Though silence has a bitter taste in
self-defense or battles faced
often words we speak in haste destroy love...
what a waste!
Can I tolerate this habitat I've lived in all my life?
Can I stand the imperfections
of my husband or me, his wife?
If I can search my inward thoughts
and believe in who I am?
Can I trust and act on instinct
and doing everything I can?

If I could truly know myself
and love the best in You,
then temperance would display itself
in tolerance and love too.

LORD, HELP ME LOVE & FORGIVE

Lord…You say in Your Word to forgive.
I'm ashamed because I don't know how.
The way I judge is the way You'll judge me
and the things I permit…You, too, will allow.

So please help me learn to love and forgive
the way You did and expect of me.
I'm aware that Your image is not in my mirror
and I don't reflect You for others to see.

I know that love is a two-way street
and if I can't give…I'll never receive.
When vindictive people start to attack
I try hard to love, but it's make-believe.

Their actions are malicious and spiteful
devoid of charity…they are just plain mean.
They cheat, they steal, and lie about others
while their inside persona remains unseen.

I'm not very good at play-acting.
It's a waste of time…for You see my soul.
So I'm thinking the only way out for me
is for You, "Yourself," to take control.

It's true that I'm free, and my will is my own
but unforgiving keeps my poor soul bound.
I recite Your Commandments…and try to pray
but my will stays unyielding on this battleground.

Lord, if I can't forgive…neither will You.
Please help me this time with my will
and help me improve at loving others
and give me forgiving skills.

HUMILITY

You're simply not born with humility,
it's something you must acquire.
Humility is worn—but is hidden,
not apparent in your attire.

Situations make it apparent
for no arrogance surfaces here
In a steadfast, unassuming nature
lives meekly without fear.

Some people try hard to be humble,
bow their head and speak very low
proclaiming submissive peacekeeping,
but exalted humility continues to flow.

You just can't put on humility,
it's something that grows from within
for a colossal ego that is selfish and smug
cannot condescend in the end.

Pre-eminence will always kick in—
their supremacy they must reveal.
Seizing authority to control the conditions
while their vanities they try to conceal.

Oh, God, help us all with our nature—
Help us control that beast within.
Learn to be loving and authentically kind
Become humble before the end.

BEWARE OF THE POT-STIRRER

Beware the approach of a gossip,
it is likely they're looking for dirt.
Pretending to be a peacemaker,
without concern for hurt.

Pot-stirrer is a name for a troublemaker
a person always stirring the pot.
They approach under the guise of friendship,
but it's likely that is one thing they are not.

Gossips enjoy the misfortune of others,
big problems are a pleasure to them.
Their pulse may race and their ears perk up.
Get ready! Get set! Condemn!

From a gossip the whole truth is seldom told,
imaginations can weave a story neat,
rehearsing and rearranging pieces
of a story they heard on the street.

The gossiping tongue spreads deception
by embellishments on a grain of truth,
slaughtering the reputations of others,
destroying lives without proof.

It's the truth that sets us free,
and peace comes when we finally see.
It was Jesus who came to point out the way
with His Life absolutely sin-free.

If the Pot-Stirrer stopped his gossiping,
repented to God and really tried,
started encouraging rather than discouraging,
harmful gossip would die.

BETWEEN YOU & ME

Sometimes Your face is hidden, Lord,
by my thoughtless, cynical heart.
I have erred. I'm that wretched offender.
But restore me in mercy. Don't set me apart.

Lord, it's so easy to become self-righteous
By condemning others only tolerant of me.
Today I feel only shame and sorrow
as I come before You on my knees.

Deliver me, Lord, from selfishness…
from proud thoughts and vanities.
Point out evil that is posing as good.
Almighty God, have mercy on me.

I know I'm my own worst enemy,
so keep my soul under lock and key
For I willfully fight for my own way,
then secretly hope that You didn't see.

It is hard to believe I do such things,
for I want my soul to be free
Help me see myself as You do,
and keep this between You and me.

If You will forgive me and keep it secret,
for it serves no purpose for others to see,
and if You don't expose me, neither will I,
and we'll work on it, just You and me.

I'm ashamed that I don't know my failings,
so quickly expose them for me to see.
Those contemptible acts that I'm capable of
or horrid thoughts that are harbored in me.

Forgive who I am and the things I do.
Enlighten my mind so I can live free.
Don't let my soul stay in evil darkness
and keep my faults between You and me.

DEAD ABOVE GROUND

Have you watched a person lose control
with a life filled up with stress,
with their mind and body failing
and escape has no access?
How do you view the simple mind
as others smile and wink,
the confusion of the aging
struggling hard to think?
It's been said it's simply natural
when the memory starts to fail,
that the old ones find it hard to focus
and lose their way in life's detail.
Are they guidelines for prevention,
stopping this failure before it starts,
or ways to avert the obvious ending
in this torture of an aging heart?
Decisions were made and wills were signed
when things seemed clear as a bell
Some appointed others to manage their life,
binding there hands while they walk in hell.
Their mind works like an electrical short
in a light that flickers in and out,
coherent twenty percent of the time,
and then begins the fading out.
I have known so many people
who were dead above the ground.

Some were even robbed and cheated,
unaware of who was around.
Humans by nature are quite greedy,
at times indifferent and unkind
Their true compassion hidden, Lord,
and kindness and pity hard to find.
Most people want to care—but don't
and still they think they do.
They pleadingly say, "Just trust me.
I'll only do what's best for you."
It's a truth of reality hard to see
when others shake their head and smile.
Maybe all of us should consider more
just how we'll walk that final mile.

I'VE DANCED OFF
WITH ANGELS

Dear ones, don't mourn for me.
I've just left a frightening place.
That place of confusion and shadows
where things I touched, I misplaced.

My body had ceased to support me,
my mind unreliable at best.
I could go on, and on, and on
but it seems I've forgotten the rest.

My heart desired to be perfect
or close to what I should be.
I never wanted to fail anybody
on my wonderful family tree.

Because I, myself, was a mortal
and the hand of flesh always fails.
I found it hard to handle frustration
when my dreams became fairytales.

I am truly thankful for your kindness
some of them great and some small.
But nothing is small when it's done in love
and if I could, I'd list them all.

I'm telling you each that I love you, and
remember, you were dear to my heart.
Your love was all that I really needed,
it filled my life from the start.

Don't cry for I've danced off with angels
to sleep, to rest, and dream.
Then I'll wake and be with King Jesus,
who my tarnished soul has redeemed.

FEEL WHAT WE THINK

Our thinking controls our life
and changes our mood in a blink.
Our disposition is mostly deliberate
and through emotion we feel what we think.

If the thoughts that I think seem hopeless,
I can be overwhelmed in a blink.
I will feel life is not worth the living,
for my mind lets me feel what I think.

If I only remember my failures
ones I can't change even if I rethink.
I start feeling sad, and depression sets in
and my mind lets me feel what I think.

When bills stack up higher than money
and my stretching has caused it to shrink,
I may feel defeated and want to give up
for my mind lets me feel what I think.

When I can't do what others do simply,
I feel brainless and my confidence sinks.
When I don't do a thing 'cause I'm overcome,
in that stupor I feel what I think.

When troubled, don't look on the bad side,
find some resolve and stay in the pink.
Negative thoughts make our mind lethargic
and attitude affects what we think.

In the morning when thoughts start to surface,
some pleasant and others may stink,
smile at the good ones and rearrange the rest,
for our brain lets us feel what we think.

Now God wrote the manual on mankind.
Jesus lived it, for He is the missing link.
We were given a free will and an excellent mind
and emotions to feel what we think.

THE HARDEST PRAYER

The prayer that is hardest to pray
is asking for the things I need.
Like the trials it takes to keep me strong
for I'll need help if I succeed.

I know I must feel sorrow some
if I would learn to care.
It takes failures to learn humility,
and be ready then to share.

I need laughter, joy, and happiness
and loved ones who want to stay.
My desire and faith is needed
when I bow my head to pray.

I need folks who are faithful
and will plant kindness seeds,
and at least enough money
to meet all my needs.

I'll need strength and courage
to help me get through,
and keep an unchanging mind
that is focused on You.

Still it isn't hard to pray the prayer
that covers all I really need,
like asking You to keep me close
and to always take the lead.

LORD, TEACH MY CHILDREN

Lord, teach my children truth
and ways that are Your very own,
and let them understand Your ways
while walking paths that are unknown.

Show them the way and light a path
for their wandering, faltering feet,
then reveal Your truth that they might feed
their hungry soul on manna sweet.

Make them strong so they may stand
upon Your Word and trust in Thee,
and let their ways reflect of You,
while living in life's troubled sea.

Lord, guide them by Your mighty hand,
and feel the love that You impart,
and let understanding drive away,
any darkness in their heart.

Give Your own sweet rest to them
that they may live empowered,
wrap each of them in love and peace
and hold them through each needful hour.

Cleanse their heart and fill them up
with goodness till they overflow,
and let their thoughts and words express
their love and their devotion show.

I thank You, Lord, for keeping them,
and allowing them to know You care,
for every time they called on You,
You were always standing there.

IS IT CHARITY OR CONDESCENSION?

Am I putting on charity or condescension?
In my head these words would chime.
The question was all about me...not God.
Will the answer come in time?
I was trying to judge and condemn,
express an opinion, then ridicule
control conditions for myself and others,
struggling for power to rule.
Though men speak with tongues
of men and angels
and have hearts with no charity,
they're as sounding brass or a tinkling cymbal.
Oh, Dear Lord, "How do You see me?"
God's Word commands us all to love
and treat everyone the same.
Jesus loved and embraced even Judas,
and I'm falling so short...it's a shame.
Still as I watch others put on charity,
pretending is what it seems to be.
I wonder, *Could I have misread their actions?*
But it feels so condescending to me.
When I see deceitful actions of others,
my wish is to tell them a thing or two.
But then I hear this voice softly whisper,
"Don't you judge them. It isn't the thing to do.

For charity suffereth long
and charity envieth not
Charity vaunteth not itself
and is never ever puffed up.
Let yourself feel some genuine pity.
You can see for yourself they are deceived.
They are victims of misinformation
and lacking of knowledge
they should have received."
My soul's enemy pointed out their failings
using my mouth for his speech.
"Oh, Lord, I've been wrong. Please forgive me.
Help me live an example I don't have to preach.
With Your help I'll live each day and keep trying,
accept Your correction, then move along.
I'll fill up my heart with real compassion,
and let You judge what is right or wrong."

LOOK FOR THE KEY

God fashioned and brought forth life
into man, beast, plants, and trees.
The Creator of all Heaven and Earth.
The Beginning. The End. The Key.

All men experience defeats and victories
for no man's life is trouble free.
But the souls who weather the wildest storms
have learned where to find the key.

No problem on earth defeats or destroys
a child of God on his knees,
while he is trusting God for protection
and is patiently waiting for the Key.

When you feel beaten by life's troubles
and your end seems like a mystery,
remember, God knows every problem
and is trying to show you the Key.

When uncertainty becomes unbearable
like howling winds or a raging sea,
God does not close or open a door
until He has given you the Key.

The Lord will not fail to be with us
He lived a pattern for us to see.
He died to bring that truth to light
and the truth of His life is the Key.

HAVE I SEEN TOO MUCH?

Have I seen too many storms in life
turning peace into disaster?
Those folks I thought could never fail
cause many to doubt You, Master.

Ministers like meteors fall,
invisible streaks of dying fame.
Lustful men have fleeced the flocks
with faces that show no shame.

Churches are weakened by disease
by the doctrines of an arrogant man.
Some faithful lose their faith and doubt
those truths whereon they need to stand.

Good ethics plummet or take to wing
and morals go belly-up.
While good marriages end up on the rocks
losing forever that loving cup.

A young, free spirit becomes enslaved
by a wolf, a showy flash in the pan.
And vulnerable souls sadly fall away
in those doubting seas or sinking sand.

Still, how could Your faithfulness be forgotten,
or the peace and love You provide.
Lord, give us courage to face these times
as our faith and beliefs are tried.

BEAUTIFUL TESTING GROUND

It's a beautiful place You've created, Lord,
for my soul's own testing ground.
It's hard to long for Heaven
with so much beauty around.

I stepped into an early sunrise,
it was so soft and still.
The snow was falling without a sound
in feather flakes on my beautiful hill.

No birds were singing or flying around,
no animal made a sound.
It seemed you could feel the heavenly silence
lingering near the ground.

Oh, it's such a winter wonderland,
though beauty is always on loan.
So I will enjoy each season passing
and the beauty that is all its own.

MY WINDOW VIEW

Such beauty I see through my windows,
with so many colors changing on cue.
A soft gray sky through the heavy mist
coloring the setting with dazzling hue.

A white-tailed deer scampered over the hill
then paused and looked side to side.
I'm envious of his grace and freedom
as behind my windows I hide.

With Mother Nature in charge of the season
encouraging the plants to grow.
She painted with so many shades of green,
it's a kaleidoscope waving to and fro.

A lighting system switches on in each plant,
blinking a message for all to see.
I've been asleep, all dry and brown.
Now I'm awake. Make room for me.

SEEING IS WORSE THAN BEING

Sometimes seeing is worse than being.
Each day these words are confirmed.
As I watch others struggle hopelessly,
knowing it is probably long-term.

Sometimes seeing is worse than being,
like when I watch my kids in pain.
Wanting to help them but being unable,
Why, it nearly drives me insane.

My desire is to show them I care
when others are doing them wrong.
That they feel my love surrounding them
when they're feeling sad and alone.

I feel my heart screaming out my love,
but my screams are lost inside me.
I watch as they try to hide their problems,
but the pain they suffer I still see.

So I sit, I hurt, I cry, and I pray.
I watch as they struggle with life.
I see obstacles cause defeat.
I feel their burdens and strife.

It's true. Seeing is worse than being.
So I pray, "God, take them in Your arms.
Cover them with Your wonderful love
and in mercy keep them from harm."

BEAUTIFUL VIEW

I look out my window each morning
over hills that stretch out for miles on end.
Each slope of one covers parts of another
one foreground stops and a new one begins.

Those hills are a little like living life,
constant beginnings and wavering ends.
Each year of living enlarges my past,
and as time passes on, the future begins.

Each year is a container of memories,
private pictures painted in the mind.
Each painting is uniquely different
with stories of individual rhyme.

My heart full of love I offer You, Lord,
for the beauty of my window view.
For as nature is painting her picture of You,
Your love for me comes through.

NO GUARANTEES IN LIFE

Life doesn't come with guarantees.
Can you afford to pay your loss?
Can you pay additional charges
if accomplishments come with a cost?

There is nothing fair in this life
and lessons don't come that easy.
Sometime the world spins round so fast.
You're intimidated and queasy.

Though persistence will keep you floating,
and your prayers light a pathway true,
the world will never meet you halfway,
it is older and tougher than you.

So take large doses of faith in your mind,
with a determined, unwavering plan.
Fill your heart with love and confidence,
and keep trying and know that you can.

A HEAVENLY MORNING

This morning holds heavenly beauty.
What my eyes see I can't describe.
It sends chills running through my body
and gives me the feeling I'd like to fly.

The ground is covered with ice and snow.
Pure white…it looks so clean.
I'm sure there have been lovelier pictures
but none that I've ever seen.

All around the morning was crisp and cold.
I awoke to this lovely winter freeze.
The snowy frost covers weeds and grass
and glistens on the ice-covered trees.

The friendly fields all sparkle like diamonds
all glassy as they twinkle at you.
A white coat covered the scars of the land
man's junk and cluttering too.

My life holds many beautiful memories.
Each one is a work of art.
These days of frozen ice and snow
will become a memorable part.

MY HILL

I love to walk the mornings still
and touch the splendor of my hill.
One with God, trees, rocks, and land.
God's own green earth on where I stand.

My peaceful hill is my retreat
where I run to hide after defeat.
God mends my soul so I can live,
while comfort to my heart He gives.

It is not hard to bend my will
in the tranquility of my hill.
Where God abides and bids me stay
and keeps His child made out of clay.

My Lord, the lover of my soul
surrounds me by His love, I know.
He'll never leave me. I need not fear.
On a cross He died to make that clear.

When shadows linger dark and near
and distress reduces me to tears,
He brings me peace and serenity
by walking my peaceful hill with me.

Lord, if I walk my hill in care,
please always let me find You there,
as I feel the wind blow on my face
and rest in Your amazing grace.

OBEDIENCE

It's my duty to be submissive to God
and ready to answer His call.
Not to question everything I see
and obey His Commandments, one and all.

But I see all the throw-away people,
called the "Trash of Society."
It seems that the world can't see them,
but it isn't the same for me.

I see broken-hearted children crying
and a mother abandoned, alone...
a man forsaken and defeated and some
elderly who have no home.
Father, I know this isn't your doing,
but I'm sure that You must see
dreadful conditions painting pictures...
pictures distressing to me.

God's people are the salt of the earth
and should lighten the load of the poor.
It seems the salt has lost its savor,
to be trampled underfoot evermore.
Lord, I've been thinking about forgiveness
that all my failures need.
I lack faith, trust, and obedience...
ingredients I need to succeed.

My senses strive to direct.
They control me by what I see and hear.
I'm driven like all the other people,
living lives bound up in fear.

I think I pretend not to notice.
If I do not acknowledge, I don't have to see.
Besides, if others knew my failings,
they would never pardon me.

Can I take that first step of faith
and understand that God will never reject?
Then love this pitiful, broken person,
show God's love, and His love accept?

I must remember the words of my Savior
and the insight He put in my heart.
To accept the truth and stand on faith,
with obedience being the principle part.

HIS UNSEEN PRESENCE

You ask me what force commands me.
What drawing power directs my way.
Why I have faith in what I can't see,
and why am I comforted when I pray.

There's an unseen presence around me,
and that presence influences my ways.
Those ways make my life more controllable
and give peace each and every day.

Sometimes I have wondered if it's an illusion
and in doubting, I ask, "How can this be?"
When a voice beyond all natural hearing
says, "It's spirit, not flesh that you see."

I keep in mind what Jesus promised,
the "Comforter," He said He would send.
It is the life of God and His warming nearness
that strengthens believers from deep within.

The Comforter performs God's will on earth,
then we understand more than the human way.
So we can absorb God's food for our soul,
giving meaning to all He had to say.

God's Word and Spirit comfort me.
The power of Christ's Life speaks the same.
Jesus is God's Christ...Today and forever.
My prayer is I always live in His Name.

WHAT IS A MAN?

What is a man that of him You are mindful,
or his children that you let them see?
What's in a man that You should love him,
and what do You see in me?
What is required of me, Lord?
What is the job You would have me do?
How can a spirit that is trapped in a beast
interact with Holy and relate to You?
Lord, You were born in a beastly body
just like me…it was Your natural life.
Like me, You were helpless as a baby
and grew up overcoming trouble and strife.
Lord, as I look at Your birth and life
and records You left me to read.
Recorded proof You were first partaker.
You suffered it all. You took the lead.
You're the author and finisher of my faith.
You performed Your mission unflawed.
Endured the cross, despising the shame,
now You are at the right hand of God.
Don't let me hate Your chastisement.
Let me keep in mind I am Your child.
Always remembering chastisement in love
is needful…if God and I reconcile.
Let me live holy and in peace with all men,
if I can't I may not see God.

Keep me steadfastly on Your path,
and in safety and peace let me trod.
Don't let my flesh defile Your mountain.
Don't stone me or thrust me through with a dart.
Help me embrace what You command
and achieve the desire in my heart.
Let me truly understand Your purpose.
How in love Your power is concealed.
How in brightness of glory You came down
and God's likes and dislikes You revealed.
You taught us God's Holiness and Power
that His righteousness purges our sins,
that the Church should be the image of You
to gain God's favor and win.
What is a man that of him You are mindful,
or his children that You let them see?
What's in a man that You should love him,
and Lord, what do You see in me?

LORD, HELP US ALL

My Lord and my Heavenly Father
who created this world and me,
I pray You care for those I love
and allow Your angels to oversee.

Give us things that are good for us
and help us to love one another.
Make our fathers godly men
and our women loving mothers.

Watch our children everywhere
and keep them safe from danger.
Help them grow up strong and good,
learning to love and bypassing anger.

I thank You, My God and my Father,
my Savior, my Lord, and my Friend,
for all the love You have given me,
from my family and others you send.

Lord, let me always be kind and good
and be there for a sister or brother.
May I never offend a hurting child,
but nurture them as a mother.

I thank You, Lord, for staying with me
through the darkest night till break of day,
and for being my ever-present help,
and giving me strength to work and play.

Forgive me, Lord, for those things I do
that are not kind and good.
Forgive me when I fail you, Lord,
and help me be the way I should.

LOVE AGAIN AND AGAIN

When you're looking for love,
try searching your heart,
though you say you've tried
and can't seem to start.
There were times you committed
but your heart got torn.
You gave all you could then had to give more.
Those you loved didn't love you,
could not fill your need.
Your honesty scared them or
they paid you no heed.
Your heart would be broken
or shrouded in fear.
Your feelings were silent, vague, and unclear.
Well, don't falter. Keep trusting.
Keep love in your heart.
Love yourself and then others,
for that's where it starts.
Your pain and rejection will diminish someday.
For time heals all wounds, just mark what I say.
Look deep in your heart.
Close your eyes and listen.
Learn from your own pain and
hot tears that glisten.
Make friends with yourself,
then go search for the truth.

Restrict time you waste,
it consumes all your youth.
Anticipate triumphs of impending days,
then keep trusting love, or the piper you'll pay.
Fill your days with sunshine or maybe some rain.
Enjoy all the pleasure and suffer the pain.
Throw open the windows and let feelings in,
for love without feelings will never begin.
You're never alone, for God's by your side.
Life is packed full of wonder
and filled with surprise.
Love again, again, again, and again.
Let friendship and love your confidence win.

THE SERPENT'S VOICE

It's recorded that God made the serpent
more subtle than any beast of the field.
Eve listened to the serpent's voice
and that's when man's fate was sealed.

The serpent is the carnal mind
and dust—the earth after God's removed.
God's link to the serpent was broken
when his way of thinking, God disapproved.

Jesus told the people who questioned Him,
"You're accountable, when you say I know."
A man's mind was made for him to reason,
but when carnal, it strikes deadly blows.

When we can identify the serpent,
perceive who he is—realize his power,
our days of childhood are then over
but our spiritual life will gain power.

Before he is named, the serpent's invisible
for Adam and Eve, and for you and me.
We're all born with a will and desire,
but controlling them will set us free.

It's not God's will to waste our mind
and become a wiggling worm.
The work of the worm enriches the earth
he just eats, expels, and squirms.

It's God's will that we learn to be righteous
and live by the pattern of His Son.
Learning that the carnal mind holds death
and the voice of the serpent to shun.

MY PEACEFUL HILLTOP HOME

I love my peaceful hilltop home
a place where God is personified.
I love being lost in the beauty of sunrise
as brilliant colors paint the sky.

I love the closing of lazy days
and blazing sunsets as night appears.
I love darkened skies and restless wind
blowing the rain that I love to hear.

I love Mother Nature changing seasons,
and she changes four times a year.
Not only does she change her clothes,
she changes the music I hear.

It's not only the beauty of the trees
or the splendor of the skies.
It's not only the feel of the misty air
or the song in the wind's reply.

In this place with God's presence around me,
I seem to hear His voice so sweet.
It is then the surrounding beauty fades
and His love makes me feel complete.

THE LEAD HORSE

The Lord owns the Lead Horse.
He is His to command.
He must know the Lord's voice
and the touch of His hand.

We must pray for the Lead Horse,
for his job is demanding.
He needs strength not to stumble,
causing misunderstanding.

The Lead Horse must hold fast,
though others won't stand,
And, in harness…wait quietly
for the Master's command.

The Lead Horse must take his
bit without champing,
though storms of life rage and
all others are prancing.

The Lead Horse must hold fast until
the Master is ready,
endure mass confusion,
but remain calm and steady.

The Lead Horse moves only
at the Master's command
even when he's not certain,
he must trust the Lord's plan.

Dear Lord, help the Lead Horse know
Your will and Your plan.
Hear our prayers for our Lead Horse,
as we hold up his hands.

Show the Lead Horse Your will,
Lord, and direct from above,
then guide and protect him...
wrap him in Your love.

PASTOR SHAW

Have you ever sat in an empty room and
wondered who you might have been?

That person no one will ever know
before God spoke or dwelled within.
Did you question if He asked too much
when His love demanded honesty?
Because only you could search that truth
and choose your destiny?
God burned away all subterfuge
and uncovered fears for you to see,
then let you look beyond yourself
before His power set you free.
Like Moses with his shoes removed
by the burning bush on Holy Ground,
your feet were placed on a righteous path
where the ways of God you found.
Your walk with God could never
have true depth or authenticity,
if you closed your eyes to faults within
or refused responsibility.
I'm glad you chose to follow God
and hold the name of Jesus high.
I'm glad you have eyes to see the poor,
and ears to hear the widow's cry.
You share our heartaches and troubles

and then you lend a hand.
The love you gave was born of God. It couldn't
have come from man.
Your ways are simple and humble,
a living soul in earthenware.
Your hand's an extension of Jesus…
manifesting God's love and care.
Such wonderful truths you have taught us,
while always instructing us to pray.
And the fruit of those prayers have given us faith
that will keep us in His way.
The fruit of our faith is acceptance
of our wonderful Savior's love,
and the fruit of His love is eternal,
bringing us God's peace from above.
I pray that God will honor you,
for the things you're careful *not to do*.
Like uncovering flaws and secret sins until
deliverance we pursue.
Your office is a lofty place and
I'm sure you feel alone at times.
May love and mercy cover you
on your demanding climb.
I thank you for all of your labors,
especially because we were never deceived.
May God bless you and keep you forever
in your struggles that only He sees.

OUR PASTOR'S LADY

You're the Lady on our Pastor's arm
full of love and passive charm.
You change the mood of our hectic day
when your gifted hands began to play.

Your music calms the savage beast
and lets our fears and troubles cease,
making it easier for a soul to find
its life source in this daily grind.

Your music beckons God's sweet light
and drives the darkness into flight.
Always remember you're in God's hands
when nothing goes the way you plan.

When you feel there is too much to do
and no one sees the hurt in you,
keep in mind God is in charge of things,
and all is well. Let the people sing.

When you're feeling down and all alone,
think you can't make it on your own,
remember gifts of God are more than pleasure
and He gave you faith…at least a measure.

In your music we feel His presence near
reminding us to have no fear.
Then our prayers are that you always hear
the Lord's voice whisper in your ear.

Remember when you're feeling weary
and the day's a little more than dreary,
it's the Lord who gives us hope and love,
sweet peace and blessings from above.

It's He who gives us worth and grace
then bids us rest in His embrace.
So don't feel scared or all alone,
you're in God's family. So feel at home.

GOD IS LOVE

I hope I never forget to remember.
Love is not a word—God is Love.
Love is not something man concocted
but the life of God from above.

Love fails or fades when neglected,
so only the foolish hearts abuse.
The unwise man distorts and perverts love,
bringing heartbreak by it misuse.

God's Love is forgiving, sharing, and caring,
being loved and nurtured by another.
It's joining hands. It's heart-to-heart.
It's uplifting the hands of a weaker brother.

The perfect life we all want and dream of
is a life of happiness and peace.
Those sharing love that is unending
discovered by giving…it will only increase.

The source of eternal love is God and
His love patterned our love for each other.
The power that nurtures faith and trust
dissuades dishonesty to another.

Lord, teach our hearts Your ways of love.
Don't let it continue to confuse.
Love is not something man produces.
It's Your life and Love we're allowed to use.

LORD, IT'S JUST ME

Almighty God...My Heavenly Father,
it's just me again, but nevertheless,
I need to be wrapped in Your gentle arms
and covered by love in this cold darkness.

Forgive me, Lord, for the things I do
that displease or make You sad.
The desire of my heart is to please You, Lord,
but my good intentions often turn bad.

Renew Your spirit in me each day,
put love in this heart of mine,
and let it be filled with selflessness
and concern for all mankind.

Keep my mind in remembrance, Lord,
of the mercies you have shown to me,
and never remove the light from my path,
but continue to let me see.

It's those glimpses of glory You have given me
that spark, my desire to try again.
The flush of shame that prompt my conscience
or a harsh correction now and then.

Today I'm feeling so flawed and unworthy
before one so gracious to me.
Please remind me, Father, of Your will for my life
then to help me fulfill it is my plea.

LIFE TRIGGERS CHANGE

All setback**s** in life trigger change
and those days may be laden with strife.
Those big plans you made that seemed so good,
time and chance may have changed overnight.

Nothing in life comes without doubt
and nothing is appointed to everyone.
Few are recipients of family wealth,
and none are assured that trouble won't come.

Still there is one thing you can count on,
God's love and mercy will see you through.
When storms wash away your charted path
another passage will open for you.

Or maybe God will send an angel.
If so, take care what you say or do.
For if they are there to lend a hand,
they are acting on God's love for you.

Looking back on life, have you wondered
why things rarely went as you planned?
Remember when your dreams did crumble,
He never let go of your hand.

Sit back and reflect on your yesterdays
all those memories of faraway times.
Consider how God sent solutions
or opened doors that you couldn't find.

When you were forsaken by fair-weather friends,
remember the Lord was the friend who stayed.
With arms that were ready and waiting,
He was always a prayer away.

So when you are reduced to your lowest level,
defeated and thinking you just can't cope,
remember the Lord keeps all His promises,
and all those promises are filled with hope.

TRUTH AND REALITY

The real truth is always the truth
and no one can have their own version.
A version we try to sell to each other
in numerous ways of coercion.

We must learn to make truth and reality checks
and examine our words and our actions.
It's easier to dream and pretend through our life
for in dreams, we're insured satisfaction.

The real truth is always the truth
though its harshness may cause some aversions.
Some folks try to change the face of the truth
by meaningless words on elusive excursions.

The truth isn't changed by our unbelief
or a point of view we can't see.
We can dream and pretend as much as we like
but in real truth…there's truth and reality.

GIVE ME FAITH TO HAVE FAITH

Lord, give me faith to have faith
when my life appears to be shattered.
Help me have faith that rightness reigns
when all of my plans are broken and scattered.

Give me courage when my heart is breaking
to press forward and truly forgive.
Give me the boldness and strength that it takes
to labor, sustain, and to live.

Let me acknowledge to You my transgressions
then reveal any hidden sins.
For You, my Lord, are my hiding place
my ever-present Savior and Friend.

Help me have faith, Lord, when stars are dark
and truth on earth doesn't seem to abide.
Help me have faith that You are in charge
and faith that You'll walk by my side.

TAKE TIME

Take time to examine the way that you live.
Take time to love one another.
Take time to encourage your sister each day
and give a hand to a brother.
Help the children of God
and caution the weak not to stray.
Live the pattern Christ lived for you.
Let your life be a picture
that He's walking through.
A critical spirit is helpful to none,
its damage we see everyday.
The spirit you've wounded may stumble and fall
and it might be your children you slay.

GOD'S GIFT OF LOVE

Man is a self-willed creature
that God to life did bring.
He placed him in a garden fair
where plants bloom and creatures sing.

He was made in God's own image—
the image of Him true and bold.
God breathed in him the Breath of Life
and man became a living soul.

God took a rib from Adam's side,
made a woman—flesh and bone.
Then things went so very wrong,
Eve let the serpent into their home.

God drove them from their garden—
East of Eden, the cherubim's site.
With flaming swords that turned each way,
they were to guard the Tree of Life.

The ground was cursed for Adam's sake
and sorrow to Eve and her seed.
The serpent was cursed above all cattle
and dust would be his feed.

Two sons were born to Adam and Eve—
two characters rooted deep.
Cain was a tiller of the ground
and Abel, a keeper of sheep.

The brothers gave offerings to the Lord.
Abel's firstling had God's respect.
Cain presented the fruit of his field,
but his offering God would reject.

Cain killed Abel as they talked in the field—
his malice and rage were vicious.
Abel's blood cried out from the ground—
the picture was more than suspicious.

To Cain, God said, "Where is your brother?"
He answered, "Am I his keeper?"
God said, "Cain, you are banned from the earth
and you'll have no yield for the reaper."

Cain cried, "God, my punishment's hard—
it is far greater than I can stand!
You're gone. Your face is hidden from me,
and I'm driven far from the land!"

"On earth I'm a fugitive—a vagabond,
to slay me all men will try."
That day God placed a mark upon Cain—
protection so he wouldn't die.

Then God let flesh rule over man
and his spirit wander free.
East of Eden, in the land of Nod,
their lives persisted aimlessly.

Another good seed was given to Eve—
this fact is not a fable.
In love, God gave her another son
named Seth instead of Abel.

Now the earth was filled with violence,
and it grieved God in His heart,
but He looked down upon Noah
and decided to save a part.

The Word of the Lord came to Noah
and He told him what to do.
He said, "Make you ark of gopher wood.
Have faith, I'll be with you."

He told him just how to build it,
with dimensions strong and stout.
He said to make it three stories high,
then pitch it inside and out.

He told him to take the animals
and called them two by two.
"Take food for them, your wife,
your sons and their wives too."

Noah followed God's instructions well.
That it would rain, he had no doubt.
God called the animals to come inside,
then locked the others out.

For forty days and forty nights,
the storm tossed the ark about.
After floating a hundred and fifty days,
God's wind dried the water out.

It was a precious seed God was guarding.
In time He would set them free,
never to destroy the earth again
by the waters of life's sea.

He decided man needed lots of help
if long they would endure.
So He guided those who sought Him,
types and shadows to procure.

With stories told by a mighty God
to hearts with no restraint,
such perfect illustrations
those allegories paint.

God gave the law to Moses
and explained what had to be.
Important types for fallen man,
to set his fettered spirit free.

A faithful few are always saved
who love and honor God.
They see His ways, they hear His voice,
and find His path to trod.

The best of Heaven's treasures
is a heart that's full of love.
Heaven's greatest treasure
is sweet Jesus from above.

Peace on earth, good will to men,
the angels sang one day.
Jesus' life bought back our souls—
a debt He chose to pay.

God sent His Son into this world—
His offering set us free.
Essential gifts in changing times
are ears that hear and eyes that see.

He walked through hell to chart a path,
a pattern for us all.
Only His endless Love and Truth
could free man from the fall.

STAY PLIABLE IN HIS HAND

Stay pliable in the Hand of the Lord
Stop resisting—let Him take command.
Follow His lead without question
it's then He allows you to understand.
But don't try to give the leader instructions
report for duty…then quietly stand.
His grace will protect you wherever you go
if you're pliable in His hand.
The Lord may choose to remain concealed
but your soul will realize that it is Him.
So keep yourself ever alert and ready
and don't give in to your own whims.
Ears to hear and eyes to see are needed tools
and are gifts from the Lord.
And when you can detect His presence
you're driven by love not reward.
A human can't understand God's love
or comprehend His ways and speech.
We choose to listen to a world full of voices
chattering voices that never bring peace.
The world is full of pain and confusion
it's noisy and filled with so much strife.
God can teach more in one moment of silence
than chattering voices will all of your life.
He won't force you to choose his way
it's your call to choose what you do.

But if you're sensitive and listen to Him
His Spirit and Word will lead you.
Don't be afraid, or resist His voice,
when He speaks you'll know it is He.
For He has delivered you so many times
and it's not a stranger's face you will see.
So rest pliable to the hands of the Lord.
Don't resist…for He has a wonderful plan.
Follow God's lead and give Him your heart
and trustingly take His hand.

THINK IT THROUGH AGAIN

Young women beware…consider your thinking
the time on your hands you're starting to see.
You've many jobs left and your mind keeps asking
if a mother and wife are what you want to be.
Your days and years have melted together
they're lost in the muddle of your imagery.
While fictional memories meander around
where boredom begets its own destiny.
Resenting the days of unending labors
your conscience holds on to its own sanctity.
Look into your heart and then into your mind
your husband and children are what you will see.
Your station in life makes very few changes
and far away places you may never see.
You may have extracted your last ounce of effort
for the man and the babies on your family tree.
So think about places and faceless people
the amazing excitement you think it would be.
Then look in the innocent eyes of your children
depending and loving with intensity.
That heart beating in you is the heart of a mother
cooking, cleaning, and nursing each day.
At this time your dream of
dreams is with you
your husband, your home,
and your children at play.

So dream all your dreams then lean back and smile
and think of the happiness you've brought today.
Then think of the people without love or purpose
repent in your heart, bow your head, and pray.

HEART OF A HEALER

You're a doctor with the heart of a healer.
Not many doctors feel the needs.
I think God's spirit commands your actions
and directs your heart and deeds.

Sometimes it seems like an illusion
and I wonder why you're helping me.
Then a voice speaks out beyond my hearing
declaring you have eyes to see.

You're a doctor with the heart of a healer
You can calm a patient's silent screams,
by pointing out another path
and patching up their broken dreams.

You listen to the cries of children
and feel the pain in a broken heart.
You hear the fear in a dying whisper
and linger close as they depart.

You're a doctor with the heart of a healer
a role that's rare indeed.
I pray God's blessings fall around you
and in all things you succeed.

This blinded world may often hurt you.
Betraying friends may let you down
but your Friend and Savior, Jesus Christ,
will always care and be around.

As one door shuts and another opens
what lies ahead you can only guess.
Just follow the light at the end of the tunnel
and know that you've been truly blessed.

You're a doctor with the heart of a healer.
You're a friend on whom we can depend.
You're a man who understands our feelings
and love will be your dividend.

HELP ME, DOC

A nasty little flu bug crawled under my skin.
I can't even tell you where or when.
He's such a savage little critter.
He is vicious, heartless, mean, and bitter.
My head is throbbing. My stomach is sick.
It twists. It cramps. It lunges and kicks.
My fever is high, my mouth hot and dry.
My face is burning. I want to cry.
I lose my food in various ways.
Not even a teaspoon of water stays.
I'm weak as a kitten, and all my bones ache.
I can't even move, for heaven's sake.
I tried to evict him, this unwanted tenant,
then came more nausea, I know that he sent it.
Please help me, Doc! This isn't much fun.
He's turned into hundreds instead of just one.
Help me, Doc!

I wrote this when I was sick with the flu and found it hard to get off the bathroom floor long enough to call the doctor. I yelled at my husband to call him for me, but he kept asking what he should tell him. That's when I wrote down my symptoms, and he and the doctor found it hard to take me seriously after they had heard my complaints.

THE GOAT & THE ELECTRIC FENCE

Our billy goat thought he was "King of the Hill"
and he sure liked to push me around.
When he'd lower his head and charge,
if I wasn't careful, I'd be on the ground.

He didn't like me, and I liked him less.
We fought major battles I'll never forget.
He wouldn't change and neither would I,
so we fought at sunrise and sunset.

Every morning when I'd head for the barn
to milk the cows and feed the stock
Old Billy would meet me down by the gate
blocking the path where I had to walk.

He'd rear up tall and come down hard,
snort and shake his head and cough.
I'd jump on his back and he'd head for the barn
and run under the corn crib to knock me off.

But before he could drag me under the crib
I'd stand on his back and climb in the loft,
then he'd run under, then turn to butt me
and seeing me gone, he'd grunt like an oaf.

Then one day our battle was different.
I arrived at the gate and he wasn't there.
So I started to walk to the barn by myself
   'cause I didn't see Billy anywhere.

The grass was wet and lazy looking.
It had rained and the sky was grey and blue.
The cows were still lying in the stable.
Lord knows I wanted to stay in bed too.

My eyes were scratchy, my vision blurry,
   my brain was fuzzy at best.
The light was dim and full of shadows,
but I noticed the old bull looked stressed.

The goats were still huddled under the barn
and the old sow grunted as she stood up,
disturbing her pigs and they started squealing
and ran for the trough without washing up.

The rooster crowed, the hens scratched for seed,
and Old Tommy Turkey wanted to fight.
Old Tom is alive 'cause he's too tough to eat,
   so he struts all day until night.

The fence around the barnyard was old,
   but was reinforced by electric wire.
It had one string high and one string low,
   they were attitude adjustment wires.

It didn't take long until everyone learned
if they stayed off the fence it was better.
For a battle with Dad's old electric fence
caused me pain and made the ground wetter.

I felt smug as I climbed up the hill.
I thought maybe Billy had finally learned
if I did the feeding…I was boss,
but a rustling noise caused me to turn.

Here came Old Billy bucking and snorting
I am sure that I saw him smile.
I headed back to the fence for protection,
and the distance back seemed like a mile.

I prepared to jump on that last long step
and up in the air my body flew high.
I thought I had made it to safety at last,
leaving Old Billy high and dry.

But, Lord, when I felt my jeans hit the wire
and those tingling barbs pierce my skin,
with one foot in the air and one in the water,
both of us knew it's the fence that would win.

Inspiration, Reflections, & Love

THROW CAUTION TO THE WIND

I'm at the point of no return
if you can't teach an old dog new tricks,
if I can't keep the wolf away from my door,
I might as well hit the bricks.

I will hold my horses while I hold the fort
though my heart is my mouth,
for I've lost all my money and common sense,
why heavens to Betsy, it all flew south.

Now I'll lay all my cards on the table
and won't take any wooden nickels,
take the bull by the horns through thick and thin
while my feet are as cold as icicles.

I went for broke—got an ace up my sleeve
and I made it by the skin of my teeth,
then I came up smelling like a rose
and sitting in the cat-bird's seat.

I've given up being down in the mouth,
I refuse to be down in the dumps.
If worse comes to worse in this old life
I'll just stand up and take my lumps.

I know every cloud has a silver lining
and it's darkest before the dawn.
So I'll keep on flying by the seat of my pants—
call all the shots and not sing a swan song.

I'll make hay while the sun is shining
and strike while the iron is hot,
I'll carefully hit the nail on the head
and sweet success will hit the spot.

If I hitch my wagon to a star
stick out my neck and stick to my guns,
keep a stiff upper lip and pull out the stops,
I can sing for my supper
'til the day is done.

THE PERSON I BE

"Who are you?" you inquired of me.
I said, "The one I am or pretend to be.
The one I am hides deep inside
the one that others think is me.
The one I am has found a place
that is safe from prying eyes.
A place where I am never known
by the casual passers-by.
So you're not impressed with who you see
and proceed to treat me uncaringly,
I'll just go my way—this person I be,
and you'll see the one you think is me.
How sad it is for you and me,
if the one I pretend is all you see.
A friendly rapport never can be
if you think my pretender is me."

LADY AND THE STORM

The night's stormy sky was blustery and dark
and the eyes of my lady were anxious and stark.
The tall trees and bushes were dancing again
on the verge of breaking by the driving wind.
Then out of the thunders and spattering rain
in a flash of lightning the house became plain.
My lady was wet and her harness was soaked.
My jacket was dripping. My hair was a joke.
We both hit the door at the very same time
I started to laugh without reason or rhyme.
My little wet dog darted under my feet
We both tumbled in. I lit on my seat.
Though I love watching storms
and my dog loves to roam,
when you're cold and wet, you're glad to get home.
There is beauty in the wind and restless skies
but it's best from a perch that is warm and dry.
I love a comfortable place of my own
and I thank You, God, for my hill-top home.

Inspiration, Reflections, & Love

THANKS FOR MAKING ME A MOMMA

I've roses to wear, for it's Mother's Day.
One day set aside every year.
It' a bouquet of peace and contentment, for my
children are always near.
Thanks for making me a Momma.
Of all my roles, I like it best.
You only see the good in me, forgetting all the rest.
I remember my darling little boy
and my smiling girl so sweet.
They would wrap their arms around
my neck until they fell asleep.
They both have grown past childhood
into a woman and a man.
My memories are precious treasures.
Each warm like a glove to a hand.
My mind recalls a little girl
who chattered on each day.
I'd pray she'd stop to rest her tongue
or run out of things to say.
I smile at those thoughts in this silence I'd
exchange for the sound of her voice.
For the chattering talk of that little girl
would always be my choice.
Then this little blond boy pretender,
oh, he lived in a world all his own,

playing the mighty warrior,
or a young Viking leaving his home.
He gave silly cards on my special days,
maybe bought one or made his own.
He vowed to keep me in jelly beans,
with a brush pile for a home.
No mother could have had finer children—
if she searched the world around.
For a sweeter girl or more caring boy in
this world could never be found.
Their lives have left an impact
that life cannot erase
no matter how far they travel,
or how fast may be their pace.
My children were always there for me,
in trouble, sorrow, or pain
encouraged me when hope was gone,
their love much like a summer rain.
They understood my failures and
brought out the best in me.
They held my hand in trouble until
my tear-filled eyes could see.
Now even though they're on their own
it means so much to know
their love is wrapped around me—

I can sleep in that afterglow.
Each Mother's Day is another chance
to pause and start anew.
My children add meaning to my life
and made so many dreams come true.
Thanks for making me a Momma.
Of all my roles, I like it best.
My children love and understand—
forgetting all the rest.

FATHER'S DAY

Father's Day is set aside
and you're the heir apparent.
This celebration will require some
tolerance of the parents.
This may be a blueprint for a father tried and true
so as you read it to yourself, let it speak to you.
Remember, it's a "Thank You Day"
for all the things you do,
for help in times of trouble and
giving guidance too.
Still you must show patience,
for they have so much to learn.
Don't be blind to their struggle,
it's for approval that they yearn.
Patience is the cornerstone as a father daily works.
In wisdom give attention to your
children's cares and quirks.
A father must be loving to his children
large or small.
He must use common sense
and knowledge
and be thankful for the call.
Mix lots of understanding and mercy
with your love.
Keep constant communication with
your Father up above.

Now discipline is a tricky task.
Administer with discretion.
For effectual discipline is mixed
with mercy and compassion.
Edify your little ones, they're weak and timid too.
They learn by listening to you
and by all the things you do.
Make sure the love you have for them
is active and sincere.
Let them obey because of love
and not just out of fear.
All your habits they observe.
One day may be their own.
A child is a natural mimic
and some day they will be grown.
Just remember you're their hero
and that their love is from the heart.
Their life is passing quickly,
so choose to be an active part.

HOW CAN I SAY GOODBYE?

How can I say goodbye, my love,
my companion, and my friend?
How can I bear the future
when you don't come home again?
In this world my special place
was standing next to you.
Your love—my place of safety,
you made so many dreams come true.
I pray that God will give me strength
to face each future day.
For at this moment in my life,
I don't know how to stay.
Our home is filled with sorrow,
I feel so all alone.
Cold emptiness has filled my heart
like none I've ever known.
Now you are with our Savior
and in His arms you rest,
but I am still with our family,
trying to do my best.
All my memories I will cherish
as to our Lord I pray.
I'll need great strength and courage
to live alone each day.
I cannot say goodbye, my love,
my companion, and my friend.
So I'll love you through our family
since you can't come home again.

WORDS

The power of words is amazing
whether written, spoken, or screamed.
All those words in various languages
communicate man's fears and dreams.

When folks misjudge my opinion
or don't listen, for that would take time,
in my writings I have a voice,
though my thoughts may come out in rhyme.

My writings give life to my thinking,
painting pictures that others might see.
In my words I express joy and anger,
fury, resentment, or glee.

Words are a means of transferring
to others the way that I feel.
When cruel words inflict incurable wounds,
it takes words of love for a heart to heal.

THE WIND IS A BULLY

The wind is a bully. It shoves things around—
all the trees and the shrubs
and the dust on the ground.
The tree limbs are torn off
and strewn everywhere—
the shrubs are blown leafless
but the wind doesn't care.
The topsoil is scattered in every direction
by a mischievous bully with noted detection.
You can see what he's doing—
feel him blowing around—
as this unfeeling tyrant rips up the whole town.
The bushes and the brambles
are attacked without pity—
the plants and flowers are blown through the city.
He can take off a roof or
he'll make the bells clang—
break windows and pots—just about everything.
He's the great equalizer—
he can make your heart pound—
for a castle or shack he can hurl to the ground.
Makes no difference to him
if you're rich or you're poor,
does no good to whimper when
he knocks on your door.
The wind is an escort to bring in the seasons—

part of Mother Nature—I guess that's the reason.
The wind you can watch—anymore you're at loss—
if the wind is around, the wind is the boss.
The wind is a bully, but he's friendly too.
He cools summer days and brings comfort to you.
He herds all the clouds and moves rain in and out.
He is always in charge, of that there's no doubt.
Sometimes he blows the flower's perfume
out of the garden and into my room.
He moves under bird's wings and gives them a ride,
so graceful and happy as they soar and they glide.
He's a replanting service
when he blows seeds around,
then gently transplants them
in some fertile ground.
He blows the soil dry, then he brings it a drink.
He's perplexing, confounding, confusing, I think.
He's truly astonishing, this bully and friend,
but we'll need his strange
services right up to the end.

LOOKING FOR SANTA

I was always looking for Santa Claus
and I have been for many years.
Remembering that I scared him off
fills my eyes with tears.

I was seven and my brother five
the year I did that shameful deed.
My brother asked, "Is there a Santa?"
I said, "Why no, indeed."

"Somebody made him up," I said.
I broke my brother's heart in two.
Before his eyes I smashed his dream
I had told the truth, what could I do?

So I did the best I knew to do
to try to make him smile.
He just keep looking at Mom and Dad
and cried every once in a while.

Our cedar tree had eight colored lights,
popcorn rope, and paper bells.
Shiny balls with cracking paint
Why...its beauty cast a magic spell.

When Christmas Eve finally came,
the day was filled with preparation.
My brother forgot what I had said,
caught up in the celebration.

We were making candy and singing,
baking cookies to hang on the tree,
cakes and pies on the freezer top,
it looked as if I was home free.

Dad poked his head in the kitchen,
said, "You better get in bed.
If you don't, Santa ain't coming."
But as for me, I felt no dread.

Then the sound of tiny hooves
and the clacking sound of wood
flew across the front porch.
Could it be? I bet it could!

I panicked, then I looked around.
What was that dreadful sound?
Then the truth just walloped me
as Santa's sleigh touched down.

I was under the covers in minutes.
My brother on my heels.
He said, "It must be Santa,"
and we both let out a squeal.

My mommy told us both years later
that the goats were roaming around.
They had run across the front porch,
hit the rocker, and scared the hound.

Well, that's what she believed,
and it sounded pretty good.
But she didn't know the whole truth
and I ain't telling…though I should.

I've written pleading letters
and cried a million tears,
but I ain't heard Old Santa come
though I waited all these years.

JUST BE HAPPY

Kick the blues and just be happy.
You've been gloomy long enough.
Stand up straight. Square your shoulders.
Be strong when your road gets rough.

Go wash your face and comb your hair.
Stand up tall and raise your head.
Go out and meet your battles head on.
The shame would be to die instead.

Make up your mind to just be happy.
Life's not too good at very best.
Go on about your daily business.
Those who notice won't be impressed.

Now set your jaw and make your mind up.
Don't cry those salty tears too long.
Sing your song and ignore your feelings
before your youth and beauty're gone.

You must believe if you succeed.
Defeat your loneliness and gloom.
Walk out into the sunlight quickly
that's where dreams and flowers bloom.

HIDDEN PLACES

Out of sight in hidden places
somewhere deep inside of you
is a place where one can go
to be alone and think things through.

In that place of thoughts and feelings
that storehouse of hopes and dreams,
a hideaway to restore oneself
when things aren't what they seem.

A hidden place that holds our dreams
and lots of unspoken fears.
A place to remind us of who we are
when our dreams turn into tears.

Sometimes another gets a glimpse
of fears and emotions kept in there,
those guarded feelings and uncertainties
that few are allowed to share.

Sometimes a friend brings new perspective
into that "oh-so-private place."
Then the freshness of their thinking
cobwebs and dreaded ghosts erase.

It's a needful thing, this hiding place
to think and sort and cry
but needed more is a close, close friend
who encourages you to try.

IF YOU LIVE LONG ENOUGH

You're young and you're beautiful,
but just wait and see,
if you live long enough, you'll age just like me.

Your joints will stick or crack at best.
Nothing works right and hampers the rest.

Your mind starts to leak.
Most appointments forgot.
It's hard to keep current, and you lose track a lot.

Your hair will turn grey and your face starts to sag.
You'll get spotted hands, and big veins in your legs.

Your back will pop out when you need to be busy.
If you stand up too fast, you're sure to get dizzy.

You can't sing anymore,
'cause your voice breaks up.
You'll wear glasses and soak your teeth in a cup.
Go ahead and feel pious, but your day will come.
Those sure feet will stumble.
You'll forget how to run.
Your hearing will go and your eyesight will fail.

Inspiration, Reflections, & Love • 153

Your process of thinking shorts out without fail.
Your past you'll remember, both joy and pain,
a welcoming comfort when reliving again.

You'll think of your life that flew by so fast,
then you'll have to acknowledge
your youth didn't last.

THIS WOMAN I USED TO KNOW

Long ago, I knew a young girl
who looked for truth to guide her way.
She feared those long, frightening shadows
that dread cast on her path each day.

Sometimes she walked in the wind at night
and felt the sting of the blowing rain.
Sometimes she feared she would go insane
as she hugged her pillow stained with pain.

Where is God? Where could she find Him?
Her future was cloaked in obscurity.
She longed for help that didn't come.
She found herself trapped in self-pity.

It took all her strength to stay strong
but she battled all the fates.
This sad young woman I use to know
was becoming too weak to participate.

She cried out, "I can't go on this way
with a life so empty and alone.
Has time sealed up the answers
I should know because I am grown?"

Inspiration, Reflections, & Love

In fitful sleep and an anxious dream,
she saw an eye and soul of man.
Then a silent voice saturated her mind
showing her God had a plan.

Now that young girl in that long ago
found truth that lighted her way.
In God she found peace and understanding
and His truth drove those shadows away.

SIBLINGS

Our family home had kids a-plenty.
We knew each face and name;
but we failed to know their person,
see their gifts and claims to fame.

We always noticed times of failure,
seldom noting a success.
We closed our eyes, never seeing
buried pain in their distress.

Now our past is gone forever.
We can't look back without regret.
Impulsive words and silent conflicts
painful times we can't forget.

We justified ourselves in anger
"We are right. Someday they'll know."
In that righteous indignation,
planted bitter roots to grow.

What a waste of love forgotten!
Precious memories buried deep
of happy children, playing, laughing.
Those pleasant thoughts we failed to keep.

Can we walk that passage backwards?
Can't we let each other know
that we love and appreciate them
and it's love that makes a family grow?

WHY?

Why do things get complicated
when two people try to bond?
Why is it hard to accept each other?
Why isn't love a magic wand?

Why must acceptance be withheld?
Can special attraction be explained?
Why must tears always fall in secret?
Why do we talk to hide our pain?

Can others hear a lonely heart?
Does futility ever go away?
Life is empty without acceptance
and we hide under the role we play.

Why is controlling so important?
Why do we insist that the other change?
Why can't we concentrate on the good,
leaving the rest for love to arrange?

Does acceptance only come to the privileged?
Can two people be bonded for one lifetime?
Are the ways of acceptance a secret?
How can two lovers these mysteries find?

If we could love each other as we love our self
and could see through each other's eyes,
if we could respect each other's treasures,
we would understand a protective disguise.

MY FAMILY OF SEPARATES

My family is compiled of separates,
each member unique and truly rare.
Not one can be compared to another
and duplicates aren't found anywhere.

There's no such thing as "the better one."
They are one of a kind. Each one's the best.
Each will live in their window of time
and make different choices...like all the rest.

They each have strengths and weaknesses.
A fault here and there in other's eyes.
But each of them hear their own drumbeat
and use their own words to verbalize.

Each family member is irreplaceable.
No other person could take their place
or make me smile the same in my heart
or have the same beautiful face.

In my heart they each have their own room.
Separate areas with their face on the door.
Each room is precious...a memory book
that enlarges if my memory needs more.

I love my family that is filled with separates.
I love the uniqueness that makes them rare.
I'll never compare one of them to the others
but my individual love for them I'll share.

MY MISTY MEMORIES

When my misty memory appears,
gracing the night or in a daydream,
she brightens the world around me
as she rides in on a moonbeam.

She is always laughing and full of life
I close my eyes to see her smile
and feel the peace her presence brings
and hope she will stay for a while.

Her little voice had perfect pitch
singing the songs she loved to sing
I don't expect you to understand
the peace my misty memories bring.

My Misty Missy of yesterday
in my mind's eye I clearly see
in her mismatched socks and faded jeans
running up the path to me.

Her company was always such a joy
on our trips to town and such.
She sang and chattered all the way.
To me she meant so much.

Her visits and memory comfort me
and have cheered me through the years,
for in them I can feel her tenderness
and I see her face through my tears.

MR. HUNTER

No need to ask how you're doing.
You just bagged a twenty-point buck.
You told all the boys right away
it had nothing to do with luck.
You say that you're a hunter.
You hunt for meat...not just the rack.
You say it's really not just for the trophy
but you're awake at three
and out of the sack.
Oh! I'm not saying you shouldn't hunt.
If I was hungry, I know I would.
I'm worse than a hunter. I'm a hypocrite.
I'd eat all you kill
anytime I could.
Still, buddy, who are you fooling?
And just to keep your story straight
with that tough old buck,
the only two you're fooling
are you and your dinner plate.

LIFE'S MARKETPLACE

Dear lady, with your dreams so fair
and young men as you contemplate
the kind of person you hope to find
while out there looking for a mate.

Have you thought about their behavior
and things that are important to you?
Can they give and take sharing the load,
and whose dreams will you pursue?

You need to really consider your choice
about your needs, your hopes, and dreams.
Would the two of you be equally yoked
and what about your self-esteem?

Be careful driving your ducks to market
for it makes a difference in your life.
That one you chose to share your life with
will bring you peace or cause you strife.

Don't think your love can change them.
It's possible…but don't count on that.
Their character may be cast already
and you won't get a turn at bat.

Find one who'll stay through rough waters
and be there on the other side.
Find one who will work until the end
and still be standing by your side.

Whatever your life is or may not be
pick one who'll share those times of lack,
and when your future is dark or broken,
will gladly help you build it back.

The road of life is better when shared,
for sharing makes your load lighter.
And those dreams shared in a family circle
may not be valued by an outsider.

Think about all the different points
that we have talked about,
then check off selfish and critical.
It may save pain and erase all doubt.

So, lady, as you dream your dreams
and young men as you contemplate
the kind of person you may choose
when you're out there looking for a mate.

A MOMMA-CHILD

The year was 1958
the day that followed Labor Day.
Life as she knew it made a change
for a tiny stranger had come to stay.
His arrival was a bit intense
but he brought her so much joy.
This tiny baby was an awesome wonder
to a country girl and small-town boy.
The nights were filled with fears and bottles.
She found her feet were made of clay.
But when morning came
and they both were living
she and her baby would laugh and play.
He felt small and soft as he snuggled to her
and it seemed to her as though he knew,
throughout their life in time of trouble
her love for him would see them through.
He never appeared a bit demanding
or rough and noisy as a child.
He quietly entertained himself
this gentle boy with a loving smile.
How can she show her little boy
for years have passed
and he's a man,
how much his Momma-Child still loves him
and likes to play whenever he can.